EXTREME
TRAMPOLINE

Monique Vescia

rosen publishing's
rosen central

New York

Published in 2020 by The Rosen Publishing Group, Inc.
29 East 21st Street, New York, NY 10010

First Edition

Library of Congress Cataloging-in-Publication Data

Names: Vescia, Monique, author.
Title: Extreme trampoline / Monique Vescia.
Description: First edition. | New York : Rosen Publishing, 2020. | Series: Extreme sports and
stunts | Audience: Grades: 5–8. | Includes bibliographical references and index.
Identifiers: LCCN 2019013258| ISBN 9781725347526 (library bound) |
ISBN 9781725347519 (pbk.)
Subjects: LCSH: Trampolining—Juvenile literature. | Trampolinists—Juvenile literature. |
Extreme sports—Juvenile literature.
Classification: LCC GV555 .V48 2020 | DDC 796.47/4—dc23
LC record available at https://lccn.loc.gov/2019013258

Manufactured in the United States of America

Disclaimer: Do not attempt this sport without wearing proper
safety gear and taking safety precautions.

CONTENTS

INTRODUCTION

Agymnast races down a mat, then uses his momentum to execute a series of somersaults and twists. Now imagine performing the same acrobatic moves while nearly 30 feet (9 meters) in the air above a bouncy rectangle stretched on a metal frame. On the way down, you need to land on a target area that's just 7 by 3.5 feet (2 m x 1 m), then rebound up into the air again.

Whether competing against other world-class gymnasts on regulation trampolines at the Olympics or combining awesome rebounding stunts with other activities to create thrilling new acrobatic acts, expert trampolinists risk life and limb every time they take to the air. For a stunt aired on the television show *America's Got Talent*, Canadian trampolinist Greg Roe jumped from a crane platform suspended eighteen stories above the ground. He completed a triple front flip with a twist before landing on a giant trampoline. Roe has wowed audiences in trampoline battles around the world, where athletes show off their mastery of the most insane trampoline stunts.

Trampoline tricks are truly extreme. The safety risks multiply as the gymnast's altitude increases. However, athletes continue to master their fears and face these challenges, developing heart-stopping routines that leave audiences breathless. Anyone watching YouTube videos of insane trampoline stunts can see

Despite the big dreams of its inventor, George Nissen, it took almost seventy years for trampoline gymnastics to earn its place among the Olympic sports.

how dangerous trampolining can be. But even young children can learn the basics and jump for joy at a trampoline park or on a backyard bouncer.

The modern trampoline is almost a century old. While materials and designs have evolved and safety features have improved, the basic principle of the device remains the same: a trampoline converts downward force to upward motion and allows the jumper to defy gravity. What could be more fun than that?

DEFYING GRAVITY

Human beings are earthbound creatures, subject to the force of gravity. When a person trips over a rock, she will never fall up—at least not on this planet. Luckily, our imaginations aren't limited by the same forces that act upon our bodies. We have invented ways to resist gravity and send ourselves soaring through the air, in planes and rockets—and even on a simpler device called a trampoline. When a human body becomes airborne, suddenly anything seems possible.

CURIOUS GEORGE

In 1930, George Nissen, a teenager living in Cedar Rapids, Iowa, got an idea while watching a

"Rosie" MacLennan and Karen Cockburn perform a synchronized trampoline routine at the Trampoline and Tumbling World Championships in 2011.

traveling circus. As the trapeze artists landed with a bounce in the safety net, the sixteen-year-old gymnast wondered if he could design a contraption that would let a person keep bouncing and flipping on a springy surface. He began trying to build a device in his parents' garage, using canvas stretched across a rectangular steel frame. He called it a "bouncing rig," but it was not very bouncy.

Later, when Nissen was a student at the University of Iowa, he and his gymnastics coach, Larry Griswold, began tinkering with Nissen's design. Once they had a working model, they showed it to the athletic department at the university. Gymnasts and divers quickly saw the value of training on this "bouncing rig." It let them soar into the air and safely practice somersaults and twists without having to worry about landing on a hard surface. Soon, Nissen's device caught on at other major colleges and universities.

By 1937, Nissen was traveling around the United States and Mexico as a member of an acrobatic act: the Three Leonardos. Around this time, he learned the Spanish word for diving board: *trampolin.* Nissen decided to trademark his bouncing contraption under the name Trampoline.

BOUNCE YOUR WAY TO BETTER HEALTH

After college athletic departments began using his trampoline, Nissen convinced the US military to buy the device to train divers. During World War II (1939–1945), Navy Seals used trampolines as part of their pilot training. Bouncing in the air helps simulate weightlessness. The National Aeronautics and Space Administration (NASA) has used trampolines to help astronauts prepare for the lack of gravity in outer space and for the ways their bodies might flip around inside a space capsule.

As Nissen recognized early on, the trampoline has many physical fitness benefits. Trampolining (or "rebound exercise," as it is sometimes called) builds core strength and improves balance. A 2016 study conducted by the American Council on Exercise determined that a trampoline workout burns calories and improves endurance without tiring the body the way that running does. According to NASA, ten minutes on the trampoline has the same health benefits as thirty minutes of running. It's also easier on the joints of the body. Trampolining tones the muscles, increases circulation, and improves balance and oxygen

REBOUND THERAPY

Trampolines can be used as a form of therapy and exercise for people with special needs. Autism spectrum disorder is a developmental disorder characterized by interest in repetitive behavior, difficulties with communication, and challenges with social skills. Parents and therapists have found "rebound therapy" to be helpful for children with autism. Jumping on a trampoline can be an appropriate outlet for certain types of repetitive physical behavior. It also offers a child with autism an opportunity to play with other children while improving body awareness and building muscle and bone strength.

Children with autism often learn more effectively when intellectual tasks are reinforced with physical actions. A therapist will write words in chalk on the trampoline bed and ask the child to jump from one word to another to form a sentence. Rebound therapy has also proven to be effective for adults with autism.

circulation throughout the body.

EXTREME KANGAROO

Nissen worked hard to spread the word about his invention. He traveled the world promoting the trampoline. In New York City, he bounced on a trampoline in Central Park with a kangaroo named Victoria, delighting his audience of amazed onlookers. Nissen was a great advertisement for the health benefits of his device. In 1977, when he was a very physically fit man in his sixties, he hauled a trampoline to the top of an Egyptian pyramid and did somersaults up there.

George Nissen got the kangaroo airborne by bouncing at his end of the trampoline, and then timing his jumps so they would both be in the air for this memorable photograph.

JUMPING FOR JOY

From the start, people could see the trampoline's potential for fun. In the 1950s, a market was growing for leisure activities. Fads like the hula-hoop caught on. Gas stations

WHEN PIGS FLY

Victoria the bouncing kangaroo was the first animal to jump on a trampoline, but she certainly wasn't the last. On YouTube, you can find videos of both wild and domestic animals enjoying the wonderful sensation of weightlessness that you get from bouncing in the air. Dogs, goats, cats, foxes, squirrels, and even potbellied pigs know how much fun it is to jump on a trampoline. Wildlife officials in Missoula, Montana, even used a trampoline to remove a black bear from someone's front yard. They shot the bear with a tranquilizer gun. It fell out of the tree and bounced once on the trampoline before hitting the ground. Luckily, it survived the ordeal and was later released into the wild.

installed trampolines so that kids could jump around while their parents filled up the gas tank in the family car. Middle-class people were doing well enough that they had spare time and money for family fun. Trampolines were so entertaining that people wanted to buy them for their homes. Home trampolines had to be smaller, since large rectangular trampolines could not fit in most backyards.

THE RISE OF COMPETITIVE TRAMPOLINING

College and university athletic departments were early adopters of George Nissen's "bouncing rig." In 1948, the National Collegiate Athletic Association introduced

Adeva Bryan of Great Britain competes during an international trampoline competition held in Birmingham, England, in 2011.

trampolining as a competitive event, and in 1954, the Amateur Athletic Union did the same. But outside of these academic environments, competitive trampolining had a slow start. The first world competition took place in 1964 at the Royal Albert Hall, a famous concert hall in London, England. The Trampoline World Championships attracted male and female gymnasts from twelve countries, with athletes from the United States taking home the top prizes. However, another thirty-six years would pass before Nissen's invention made its debut at the Olympic Games.

TRAMPOLINES AT WORK AND PLAY

The trampoline's potential as a source of fun was clear from the start. But it was also a useful tool. College athletic departments, the military, and the space program quickly adopted the trampoline as a training device. Over time, people began devising complex aerial maneuvers that could be performed while rebounding, and the activity eventually earned a place in the Olympic Games under the larger category of gymnastics.

THE DAWN OF THE TRAMPOLINE

Long before George Nissen's fateful trip to the circus, archeological evidence shows that humans from many ancient cultures had figured out ways of rebounding, and for a variety of purposes. People may have bounced into the air as part of a religious ritual or for more practical reasons. The Inuit people of Alaska used a circular blanket made of walrus skin, stretched taut in all directions by a group of villagers. A man in the center would bounce on the blanket, gaining enough altitude to scan the horizon for seals and other animals off in the distance. Today, the Blanket Toss is practiced only as a part of Inuit cultural festivals.

THE PHYSICS OF BOUNCING

How exactly does a trampoline work? Sir Isaac Newton (1643–1747) was an English physicist and mathematician who formulated three laws of motion to describe how a body moves through space. Newton's third law of motion (also called the law of action and reaction) states that for every action there is an equal and opposite reaction. This is what happens when someone jumps on a trampoline. The person's feet generate downward force when they push down on the bed of the trampoline. This force stretches the springs attached to the frame. Then, the springs snap back like a rubber band, pulling the trampoline bed back up with an equal amount of upward force, launching the jumper into the air. The more energy in a downward jump, the higher the jumper will soar.

At the Nalukatuk Festival in the remote city of Barrow, Alaska, Inupiaq people join in the Blanket Toss to celebrate another important cultural ritual: the whale hunt.

EARLY IMPROVEMENTS

George Nissen's first trampoline was built from a sheet stretched on a steel frame. Nissen and Griswold strapped the "bed" of the trampoline to the frame with used tire inner tubes to make their contraption even bouncier. They later swapped the inner tubes for coiled springs. Eventually, padding would be added around the perimeter of the trampoline to prevent injuries when the gymnast misjudged his or her landing.

BUILDING A BETTER REBOUNDER

Trampoline technologies have continued to advance, and as of the late 2010s, most trampolines are made from a waterproof canvas or woven polypropylene, a synthetic material. Many trampoline models now come with an attachable safety net, designed to limit injuries when properly installed. The safety net surrounds and encloses the trampoline and keeps jumpers from bouncing off onto the hard ground. Safety pads covering the springs prevent jumpers from painful contact with the metal springs.

A "SPRINGLESS" TRAMPOLINE

An engineer from New Zealand named Keith Alexander learned that many trampoline injuries happen when the jumper lands on the metal springs of the device. Alexander spent fifteen years trying to design a safer trampoline. He replaced the traditional metal springs with stretching rods made of glass-reinforced fiber plastic. These rods, which are under the bed of the trampoline rather than at the sides of the frame, compress and stretch when a person jumps. Alexander's spring-less trampoline was first sold in New Zealand in 2003. As of 2016, 25,000 Springfree™ trampolines had been sold globally.

MANY MODELS

Today, trampolines come in many sizes and shapes, including circular, oval, square, and rectangular. Mini trampolines have been developed for use as part of a workout routine. There are even floating trampolines for use on the water. Falling off a water trampoline is way more fun (and far less painful) than falling off one on the ground—unless you do a belly flop. Different models are eight- or ten-sided, or rectangular, and feature a waterproof jump mat attached to an inflatable base with metal springs. Water trampolines sometimes include a swim platform and a slide.

Backyard trampolines are usually aboveground models, which are easy to install and to move from one place to another. Most trampoline parks have in-ground trampolines. Fewer injuries occur with in-ground models because they are at floor level, but they require more maintenance than aboveground models.

THE EVOLVING TRAMPOLINE PARK

The first wall-to-wall trampoline park in the United States opened in 2004. As of 2018, according to *RePlay Magazine*, approximately one thousand trampoline parks existed around the world.

From 2015 to 2016, there were fifty million visits to trampoline parks in North America.

Today's parks are full-blown entertainment centers filled with attractions and promoting the idea of fun fitness. They have huge in-ground trampolines divided into rectangles for individual bouncers, as well as basketball and dodge ball courts where you can bounce high on a trampoline to slam-dunk a basketball. Other amenities at these parks include climbing walls, foam pits, battle beams, and glow-in-the-dark trampoline courts, plus all the pizza you can eat.

Like most physical activities, jumping on a trampoline can be risky. People have been seriously hurt and some have even died from injuries at trampoline parks. Because of this, most of these facilities require participants or their parents to sign waivers saying they understand the risks of trampolining and will not hold the owners of the park responsible for any injuries.

A TRAMPOLINE BIKE?

An exciting new hybrid trampoline sport is called trampoline bike, or "tramp bike," which began as a way for riders to practice difficult tricks to perform in freestyle BMX and motocross competitions. At the Tramp Bike World Championships, contestants perform trampoline stunts using a BMX bike frame adapted for use on a trampoline. All parts of the bike are removed except the frame, forks, seat, and handlebars. Anything sharp on the bike is wrapped with tape or covered with padding so it won't damage the trampoline bed. Unlike in traditional trampoline, tramp bike contestants wear sneakers and a safety helmet for protection.

MEGA-TRAMPOLINES FOR MEDALISTS

Rectangular, aboveground trampolines are used in competition, such as at the Olympic Games, because they are so large: 14 feet long and 7 feet wide (4.2 m x 2 m). Regulation trampolines are stronger than backyard models and are able to launch a gymnast more than 30 feet (9 m) into the air. A big X marks the center of a regulation trampoline, and a red square indicates the edge of the performance area, which measures 3 feet by 6 feet (1 m x 1.8 m). Each trampoline is surrounded by safety pads, with two spotters positioned on each long side.

WHAT TO WEAR IN THE AIR

When visiting a trampoline park or bouncing on a backyard trampoline, jumpers should wear appropriate clothing. No special athletic clothing is required, but the jumper should avoid wearing baggy pants or anything with trailing drawstrings that might cause tripping. Clothes that allow freedom of movement, such as comfortable T-shirts and athletic shorts or track pants, work just fine. Jumpers should remove any jewelry and belts and empty their pockets before trampolining. One should never wear shoes on a trampoline since they can damage the surface. Special trampoline socks have rubber-textured bottoms that help feet stick to the mat or other slick surfaces.

Competitive trampolinists wear typical gymnastic clothing: sleeveless or long-sleeved leotards for girls and women, and athletic pants and singlets for boys and men. Male gymnasts often wear long pants with an elastic

In competitions, trampoline gymnasts wear clothing that allows for free movement through each stage of a routine, like this leotard worn by Japan's Hikaru Mori at the 2018 Asian Games.

waistband and stirrups that go under the feet to keep the pant legs from riding up the shins. They also create a clean visual line that accentuates the routine. Gymnasts wear socks or slipper-like gymnastics shoes while competing.

BUILT FOR FUN AND SAFETY

Both young people and adults love jumping on trampolines, and over the years this "anti-gravity" device has been adapted for use with many other recreational activities. Trampoline technologies will continue to evolve, and new safety features will have to be designed to keep pace with these changes.

TRAMPOLINE TEAMS AND OLYMPIC DREAMS

The trampoline began as a device for training gymnasts. Trampoline parks were built where gymnasts could practice their rebounding skills, and eventually teams of trampoline athletes began competing with one another at organized athletic events. But George Nissen had even bigger plans for his invention.

TRAMPOLINE GYMNASTICS AT THE OLYMPIC GAMES

Nissen was himself a gymnast, so it makes sense that trampolining is now part of the larger category of gymnastics. High in the air, trampolinists execute many of the same movements that gymnasts do on the ground, such as somersaults and twists.

Nissen dreamed that one day trampolining would become an Olympic sport, and he lived long enough to see that dream come true in 2000 in Sydney, Australia. In the Olympic Games, held every four years, men and women compete separately in trampoline events. At this

Gao Lei of China gains altitude during the Men's Trampoline Final at the 2016 Olympic Games in Rio de Janeiro, Brazil.

competition, which occurs as part of the Summer Olympics, a group of sixteen athletes from each gender first compete in a qualifying round. In this round, they perform two routines: a compulsory one with a required series of moves performed in a certain order, and a voluntary routine, with elements selected from ten recognized skills. The scores from these two routines are added together. The eight best competitors from the qualifying round then move on to the final round. Each will perform another voluntary routine of ten elements before the panel of judges.

THE BASICS OF A REBOUNDING ROUTINE

Every Olympic trampoline routine begins with the competitor standing on the bed of the trampoline. Then the athlete begins to bounce, straight up and down, until he or she has gained enough height to perform various maneuvers high in the air. The trampolinists bounce high in the air to perform their moves. Four spotters, one on each side of the trampoline, stand ready to prevent any injuries from a dangerous fall. Thick mats called safety platforms are positioned on the floor at each end of the trampoline.

These three basic body positions make up part of a trampoline gymnast's routine:

- Straight position: A jump executed with a completely straight body, with arms kept straight and rotated from the shoulders, swinging up when the jumper rises and down when he or she descends. The knees and feet are together and the head faces straight ahead between the arms. Gymnasts use this jump to gain altitude before executing aerial maneuvers.
- Tuck position: In a tuck, the gymnast's knees are close to the body with the hands clasped on the knees, the thighs close to the body, and the calves tucked close to the thighs. The gymnast's toes should be pointed.
- Pike position: The gymnast's legs angle straight out from the body, with the legs together and the toes pointed. The legs may be horizontal or higher. The arms stretch straight out and the hands are on the legs or the feet.

WHAT JUDGES WATCH FOR

An Olympic trampoline routine has ten different maneuvers, and every maneuver has a difficulty score. The competitors submit their routines to the judges ahead of time. The competitors are judged on the difficulty and variety

A gymnast in a tuck position may have points deducted if the angle between her body and her tucked legs is too wide.

SPOTTING TROUBLE

In gymnastic training facilities and at competitions, a person called a spotter monitors the gymnast jumping on the trampoline. Trampoline spotters are often former gymnasts or coaches, specially trained to help prevent injury when something goes wrong during a routine. They must be strong enough to perform this function. Spotting carries risks, too. Breaking someone's fall from a trampoline can cause injury to the spotter.

Spotters position themselves on the unprotected sides of the trampoline. They watch the gymnast's routine closely, alert to any signs of trouble. If the gymnast makes a mistake and gets too close to the ends or sides of the trampoline, a spotter must be prepared to stop him from falling off or push him back onto the trampoline bed. Spotters act quickly to reduce a falling trampolinist's momentum by making contact with the person's chest or shoulders. Because trampolinists can also make adjustments to correct their own errors in midair, a spotter must also know when not to interfere. Until they are needed, Olympic trampoline spotters try not to draw attention to themselves.

of their routines in addition to how well they execute each maneuver and how long they remain in the air. Time of flight and the athlete's landing position after each element—relative to the center of the trampoline bed and called horizontal displacement—is determined by an electronic monitoring system.

Throughout each routine, the judges pay close attention to the gymnast's form. In all positions, the athlete's toes should be pointed and the feet and legs should be together. Arms should be held straight and kept as close to the

This athlete competes during the qualifying round at the 2015 European Games as the judges review the scores. Trampoline judges must complete a certification course.

athlete's body as possible. Finally, the gymnast must end her or his ten-skill routine upright on the trampoline with both feet firmly on the springy surface. This position must be held for three seconds or points are deducted.

ADDING IT ALL UP

In Olympic trampolining, a panel of nine judges oversees each event. Two judges watch for how difficult the routine is (the A score). The score begins at zero and increases with every difficult skill that the trampolinist performs. Men typically earn an A score between 15 and 16; women's scores usually range from 13 to 14.

Five judges determine how well each contestant executes his or her routine (called the B score). The execution score begins at 10.0 and judges deduct points for errors, such as bouncing without doing a trick. For the B score, these judges each score the trampolinist's routine. The highest and lowest scores are then tossed out. The three middle scores are added to the A score to arrive at the final number. In the final score, execution counts more than difficulty. In addition to these seven judges, there is a time-of-flight judge and a chair of the judges' panel.

SOARING SUPERSTARS

Although the trampoline is an American invention, as of 2016, the United States had yet to dominate on trampoline at the Olympic level of competition. In the Summer Games held in Rio de Janeiro, Brazil, a Belarusian athlete named Uladzislau Hancharou took home the gold medal in men's trampolining with a final score of 61.745. The silver and bronze medals went to Chinese trampolinists Dong Dong

OH, CANADA!

As of 2019, the Canadian trampolinist Karen Cockburn holds the record for most Olympic medals in this sport. In 2000, Cockburn took home the bronze medal in the first Olympic Games to include trampoline, held in Sydney, Australia. In 2004 she went on to win the silver medal in Athens, Greece, and scored another silver in Beijing, China, four years later. In London in 2012, Cockburn finished fourth, narrowly missing her chance to claim a second bronze medal in the sport. She is married to Mathieu Turgeon, another Olympic medalist in trampoline.

and Gao Lei. In the 2016 women's competition, Rosannagh "Rosie" MacLennan of Canada won the gold (her second) with a score of 56.565. Great Britain's Bryony Page earned a silver medal, and Li Dan of China took home the bronze.

MORE CHANCES TO COMPETE

Trampoline is one of four events included in the gymnastics discipline of Trampoline & Tumbling, often called T&T. Other disciplines in this category include synchronized trampoline, in which athletes perform identical routines as they soar on side-by-side trampolines, and double-mini trampoline (DMT). Smaller than a regulation trampoline, the double-mini trampoline consists of a single unit with a sloping end and a flat bed. The gymnast runs toward the sloping end, jumps on it, and than jumps again on the flat bed before executing a dismount onto a gymnastics mat. Tricks are performed during the jumps or the dismounts.

Most serious trampoline athletes set their sights on competing in the Olympic Games. Other trampoline competitions held annually around the world enable the most promising trampolinists to compete against one another, win medals, and in some instances qualify for the Olympics. These competitions include the Pan American Games, the T&T World Championships, the FIG World Cup, and the Gymnastics Trampoline World Championships.

CHAPTER FOUR

REBOUND AT YOUR OWN RISK

◻◻◻■■■■■■■■■■■■■■■■■

One reason trampolining qualifies as an extreme sport is that it can be very dangerous, especially when important safety precautions are ignored. Jumping up and down on a trampoline is fun, and so easy that practically anyone can do it. As a result, people have been slow to recognize the real risks of this activity. During the 1970s, thirty years after George Nissen patented his design for the modern trampoline, a series of lawsuits filed by people injured on trampolines forced the closure of operations at Nissen's trampoline factory.

THE NUMBERS DON'T LIE

A growing body of statistics has helped call attention to the dangers of trampolining. Between 2002 and 2011, more than one million people went to the emergency room

In this trampoline park, jumpers of all ages can have fun. Orange padding between the in-floor beds helps prevent injuries.

with trampoline-related injuries, according to the *Journal of Pediatric Orthopaedics*. Most of these cases were children age sixteen and under. According to Thomas Paper, the founder of an organization promoting trampoline safety called Think Before You Bounce, you are 200 to 300 times more likely to be hurt on a trampoline than on a roller coaster.

Because of the high rates of injuries incurred by young people jumping on backyard trampolines and at trampoline parks, the American Academy of Pediatrics (AAP) has taken a strong stance against these devices. The group advises parents against recreational trampoline use. Despite these warnings, people continue to purchase home trampolines or arrange for children's parties at trampoline parks.

THE JEOPARDY OF JUMPING

Jumping on a trampoline is more likely to result in injury than any of the following activities: skateboarding, bicycling, snowboarding, sledding, ice hockey, and football. In fact, a trampoline injury is four times more likely to send you to the hospital than if you get hurt playing football. People jumping on trampolines may be injured when they fall or land wrong or fall off the trampoline, twist a knee or ankle while jumping, collide with another jumper, or attempt a somersault.

In addition to "trampoline ankle," which is a particular kind of ankle fracture commonly seen in children who have been jumping on a trampoline, some of the most common injuries that occur while trampolining are other fractures, especially broken long bones in the legs and arms; sprains; and contusions and abrasions. Less common but very serious injuries include cervical spine fractures and spinal cord injuries, such as those sometimes sustained when jumping headfirst from a trampoline into a foam pit.

TRAMPOLINE PARKS: JUMP AT YOUR OWN RISK

As of 2016, the International Association of Trampoline Parks (IATP) estimated that in the previous year there were some fifty million visits to trampoline parks in North America. Most trampoline parks consist of a series of interconnected trampolines in a large room with padded walls. Such facilities typically include pits filled with large foam blocks, slam-dunk areas, wall trampolines, and other features.

They may be fun, but pits filled with foam rubber blocks in trampoline parks have been the site of many serious injuries.

Increasing numbers of these facilities in the United States and Canada have been matched by a big spike in trampoline-related injuries. A study published in the journal *Pediatrics* reported that between 2010 and 2014, emergency-room visits related to trampoline-park injuries increased by ten times. (During this four-year period, the rate of injuries on home trampolines remained the same.) According to this study, more serious injuries occur at public trampoline parks than on home trampolines because at these facilities, multiple people, adults and children of different ages including very young kids, are often jumping at the same time.

REDUCING RISKS AT HOME

Many insurance companies won't sell you a home insurance policy, or renew an existing policy, if your house has a trampoline in the yard. The risks of using a backyard trampoline can be reduced if people follow these basic safety precautions before they jump.

- Have constant adult supervision. Especially when younger children are jumping, an adult should always be present to help spot and to ensure the equipment is being used in a safe manner.
- Only kids over six and adults should jump. No children under age six should be allowed on the trampoline since they are the ones most often injured due to their weight and size. Statistics show that children of all ages are injured more often than adults on trampolines.
- Install a safety enclosure. Safety nets build to surround a home trampoline can limit the dangers of trampoline use. These nets prevent the jumper from falling off the trampoline bed and landing on the ground or colliding with people or objects nearby.
- Install protective padding. Padding on the metal springs and frame of the trampoline can reduce the severity of injury if a jumper lands on these areas.
- Avoid flips and somersaults. Attempting one of these moves and landing wrong can change your life forever. A failed flip may result in spinal injuries, sometimes with terrible and permanent consequences.
- Jump one at a time. The type of injury known as trampoline

A padded safety net surrounding a trampoline at an indoor park helps protect visitors to these facilities. Jumpers must also follow all safety regulations.

(SIDEBAR CONTINUED ON THE NEXT PAGE)

(*SIDEBAR CONTINUED FROM THE PREVIOUS PAGE*)

ankle is most often seen when multiple jumpers are bouncing on the trampoline at the same time. In fact, according to the AAP, 75 percent of injuries happen when more than one person is jumping on a trampoline.

- Keep off the roof. Never jump onto a trampoline from a high place, such as a roof, balcony, or the top of a wall.

Unlike amusement parks, most trampoline parks aren't heavily regulated, and safety guidelines can vary from one park to another. The equipment may not be checked or upgraded regularly. The IATP has developed international safety standards for trampoline parks, but compliance is still voluntary. As of early 2019, Arizona and Michigan were the only US states that had passed laws governing trampoline parks. Canadian trampoline parks are not regulated, though they tend to follow US safety standards.

Anyone visiting a trampoline park assumes a degree of risk. These parks require every visitor to sign a waiver, a legal document freeing the park from responsibility in the event of an injury. In addition to the safety precautions that apply to home trampolines, following the park guidelines can help prevent injuries.

CHAPTER FIVE

SOARING TO THE TOP

T hough trampolining is often seen as backyard recreation, it has grown into a major sport with top athletes. They spend countless hours honing their skills and pushing the boundaries of the discipline. These are just a few of the extremely talented professionals who have bounced their way to the highest ranks of the trampoline field.

TRAMPOLINE AMBASSADOR

No other woman has won as many World Championship titles as Russian trampolinist Irina Karavaeva, who holds twelve gold medals in the sport. Formerly a tumbler, Karavaeva began training on the trampoline when she was fifteen. In 2000, at the first Olympic Games to feature trampoline, Karavaeva won the gold medal. At the 2001 Trampoline World Championships, Karavaeva

The winner of multiple gold medals, Irina Karavaeva displays great form and technique.

CRAZIEST TRAMPOLINE STUNTS

As part of his trampoline promotion, George Nissen invented a game he called spaceball, a combination of basketball, volleyball, and trampoline gymnastics. People are still figuring out new ways to use trampolines. Daredevils and thrill seekers have combined trampolining with juggling, parkour, bungee jumping, and skateboarding. Trampoline-powered cliff diving and other dangerous stunts are fun to watch on YouTube, but many videos also show what can happen when extreme trampoline stunts go horribly wrong. Obviously, these maneuvers should be attempted only by experts.

was mistakenly awarded a gold medal for her routine, after a serious judging error. The rules of this competition don't allow scores to be changed once they are announced, even when a mistake has been made. Karavaeva chose to give her medal to her friend Anna Dogonadze, the German trampoline gymnast who should have won. FIG president Bruno Grandi then made an exception to federation rules and awarded Karavaeva the silver medal. In 2014, Karavaeva earned the Fair Play award from the Foundation for Global Sports Development. In 2017, she was named Trampoline Ambassador at the World Championships.

JUMPING TIGERS

Two Chinese gymnasts have been a powerhouse team on trampoline in the Olympic Games and other international competitions. Dong Dong took home a gold medal in

At the 2016 Olympic Games, Uladzislau Hancharou of Belarus (*center*) shared the winners' podium with Chinese trampolinists Dong Dong (*left*) and bronze medalist Gao Lei (*right*).

individual trampoline at the 2012 Olympic Games and a silver medal four years later. His teammate Gao Lei won a bronze medal at the 2016 Olympics and captured the gold (his sixth) at the 33rd FIG Trampoline World Championships, held in St. Petersburg, Russia, in 2018.

EXTREME FEAR FACTOR

In 2015, extreme trampolinist Greg Roe had the audience of *America's Got Talent* on the edge of their seats. After being hoisted eighteen stories into the air with a crane, the twenty-four-year-old Canadian planned to execute a triple front

GUINNESS WORLD RECORDS, TRAMPOLINE EDITION

The famous *Guinness Book of World Records* lists many amazing trampoline feats. Here are a few:

Most Somersaults: The record for most consecutive somersaults on a trampoline was set by Brian Hudson of the United Kingdom in 2003. Hudson flipped 3,333 times in a row.

Most Forward Flips in One Minute: In 2017, a team from Italy broke the previous record for most forward flips on a single trampoline executed in one minute. As each team member flipped, he had to end up on a small platform and remain balanced there. As each successive team member completed his flip, they stacked up into a human tower of twenty-two people, beating the previous record by six.

Most Unicycle Backflips: In 2003, Canadian Cameron Fraser successfully completed two consecutive backflips on a unicycle on a trampoline.

flip with a twist before landing on a giant trampoline. From far above, the trampoline appeared the size of a postage stamp, and the winds were high, increasing the chances that Roe might miss his target.

Roe started his trampoline training as a teen. He was National Open Champion in 2008 and placed third in the Olympic trials in 2012. But nothing had truly prepared him for the *AGT* stunt, which he performed successfully and spectacularly—to everyone's enormous relief.

A LOFTY GOAL

Watching Nicole Ahsinger soar gracefully through the air, it's hard to believe she was once a clumsy kid. Her father thought a gymnastics class would help improve her coordination, though her mother—a former artistic gymnast—worried that her three-year-old daughter might get injured. Instead, Nicole came back from her first lesson and announced, "I want to be an Olympian!"

Born in San Diego, California, Ahsinger has traveled the world to compete in both individual trampoline and synchro trampoline and finally won a spot on the US Olympic

Nicole Ahsinger soars gracefully during the qualifying round at the 2016 Olympic Games. Her lack of coordination as a child turned out to be the result of poor eyesight.

Team in 2016. At the 2018 Pan American Championships, Ahsinger earned silver medals in team, individual, and synchro trampoline.

STRIKING GOLD

Someone who rebounded into trampoline history is Rosannagh "Rosie" Maclennan. The Canadian gymnast won back-to-back gold medals in trampoline at the Olympic Games in London in 2012 and Rio in 2016. Maclennan was inspired by fellow gymnast Karen Cockburn, who went on to break trampoline medal records at the Olympic Games. The two performed together, earning medals in synchronized trampoline competitions in 2005, 2007, 2009, and 2011.

JUMPING AHEAD

Trampolinists have earned their place on the podium beside other respected Olympic athletes. Double-mini and synchro trampolinists hope to see their sports represented there one day, too. The trampoline seems endlessly adaptable and will no doubt be used in combination with exciting new activities that have yet to be invented—or even imagined.

GLOSSARY

bed A trampoline's jumping surface; sometimes called the mat.

compulsory A predesigned routine that includes specific moves required of the trampolinist.

core strength The strength of the muscles in the spine, abdomen, and pelvis that help stabilize the body.

double-mini trampoline (DMT) One that is smaller than a regulation trampoline, with one sloped end (the mount) and a flat bed.

FIG The International Federation of Gymnastics (Fédération Internationale de Gymnastique in French) is the governing organization for international gymnastics competitions, including the Olympics. FIG establishes the rules, trains and certifies judges, and determines how gymnastics competitions are run.

horizontal displacement How much the gymnast deviates from the exact center of the trampoline when she or he lands.

leotard A close-fitting one-piece garment made of stretchy fabric. Most leotards have long sleeves and cover the body from the shoulders to the tops of the thighs.

nets Mesh surrounding a trampoline to keep jumpers inside and prevent injury.

physicist A scientist who studies matter, energy, and the interaction between them.

pike A position in which the upper body is close to the legs, which are kept straight.

routine A sequence of moves (usually ten) linked together with no straight jumps in between.

singlet A sleeveless athletic jersey.

spotter A person positioned next to the trampoline to insure that a gymnast does not fall off during a routine.

springs Metal coils that connect the trampoline mat to its rails, holding the frame and mat in place.

synchronized trampolining Two people jumping on separate trampolines who perform an identical routine, executing the same moves at the same time; also called synchro.

time of flight The amount of time the trampolinist is in the air and not in contact with the trampoline bed.

tuck A position in which the gymnast's knees are bent and drawn in to the chest and the body is folded at the waist.

voluntary routine A trampoline routine where the individual elements are chosen by the gymnast or the coach to reflect the athlete's best performance; also called a vol.

waiver A legal document in which a person waives his or her right to take legal action against a business, such as a trampoline park.

FOR MORE INFORMATION

American Academy of Pediatrics
345 Park Boulevard
Itasca, IL 60143
(800) 433-9016
Website: http://www.aap.org
Founded in 1930, the American Academy of Pediatrics
(AAP) is an organization of physicians who treat
infants, children, and young adults and is dedicated
to promoting the health and well-being of every child.
The AAP has issued guidelines for reducing the risks of
injuries associated with trampolines.

Health Canada
Official Website of the Government of Canada
Trampoline Safety
Address Locator 0900C2
Ottawa, ON K1A 0K9
Canada
Email: info@hc-sc-gc.ca
(866) 225-0709
Website: https://www.canada.ca/en/health-canada/services
/healthy-living/your-health/products/trampoline-safety
.html
The Canadian government's Health Canada website
includes information on the various health risks related
to trampoline use, tips on how to avoid injury while using
a trampoline, and information regarding the lack of
regulations governing trampoline parks in Canada.

Gymnastics Canada
1900 City Park Drive, Suite 120
Ottawa, ON K1J1A3
Canada
(613) 748-5637
Email: info@gymncan.org
Website: http://gymcan.org
The Gymnastics Canada website includes information about
    various national trampolining competitions, including
    Elite Canada in Trampoline Gymnastics, Trampoline
    Gymnastics World Championships, Trampoline
    Gymnastics World Age Group Competitions (ages
    eleven to twenty-one), and Canadian Gymnastics
    Championships, an annual competition featuring
    trampolining, artistic gymnastics, rhythmic gymnastics,
    and tumbling.

International Gymnastics Federation (FIG)
Avenue de la Gare 12A
1003 Lausanne, Switzerland
+41 (0)21 321 55 10
Website: http://www.gymnastics.sport/site
The governing body for gymnastics worldwide, FIG is the
    oldest established international federation of an Olympic
    sport. The group, which oversees eight sports, including
    trampoline, has been a part of the Olympic Games since
    1896, when these competitions were revived.

United States Trampoline and Tumbling Association (USTA)
6304 Bayberry Boulevard NE
Winter Haven, FL 33881
(309) 854-2896
Website: https://usta1.org
Founded in 1971 by George Nissen—inventor of the modern
    trampoline—and his coach and business partner—Larry
    Griswold—this organization sponsors the annual National
    Championships for trampoline, tumbling, and double-
    mini trampoline. USTA also issues yearly awards and
    scholarships to athletes in these categories, including a
    Griswold-Nissen Cup Award.

USA Gymnastics
130 E. Washington Street, Suite 700
Indianapolis, IN 46204
(317) 237-5050
Website: http://www.usagym.org
The national governing body for the sport in the United
    States, USA Gymnastics was established in 1963. This
    nonprofit organization sets the rules and policies that
    govern the sport of gymnastics, including selecting and
    training the US gymnastics teams for the Olympic Games
    and World Championships. It boasts a membership of
    more than two hundred thousand athletes, professionals,
    and clubs.

FOR FURTHER READING

Carmichael, L.E. *The Science Behind Gymnastics.* Mankato, MN: Capstone Press, 2016.

Carter, Caela. *Tumbling.* New York, NY: Penguin Young Readers Group, 2016.

Coy, John. *For Extreme-Sports Crazy Boys Only.* New York, NY: Fiewel & Friends, 2015.

Gifford, Clive. *Gymnastics.* Mankato, MN: Amicus, 2012.

Guinness World Records. *Guinness World Records 2019.* Ashland, OR: Portable Press, 2019.

Mason, Paul. *Trampolining.* North Mankato, MN: Sea to Sea Publications, 2010.

Mason Crest Publishers. *Extreme Sports.* Broomall, PA: Mason Crest Publishers, 2016.

Mattern, James, and Joanne Mattern. *Great Moments at the Olympics.* Des Moines, IA: Perfection Learning Corporation, 2014.

Schwartz, Heather E. *Gymnastics.* Farmington Hills, MI: Gale, Cengage Learning, 2011.

BIBLIOGRAPHY

Bhawnani, Namrata. "Deep Thrills: The Crazy Cave Trampolines of Wales." CNN, October 16, 2014. https://www.cnn.com/travel/article/wales-bounce-below-trampolines/index.html.

Carmichael, L.E. *The Science Behind Gymnastics.* Mankato, MN: Capstone Press, 2016.

Cohen, Chris. "The Casual Olympic Viewer's Guide: Trampoline." *New York*, August 2, 2012. http://nymag.com/daily/sports/2012/08/casual-olympic-viewers-guide-trampoline.html.

Egge, Rose. "Trampolines Helping People with Autism Reach New Heights." KOMO News, July 23, 2013. https://komonews.com/archive/trampolines-helping-people-with-autism-reach-new-heights-11-23-2015.

Gifford, Clive. *Gymnastics.*Mankato, MN: Amicus, 2012.

Glor, Jeff. "Wall Trampoline: The Newest Extreme Sport?" CBS News, March 20, 2012. https://www.cbsnews.com/news/wall-trampoline-the-newest-extreme-sport.

Guinness World Records. Trampoline Records. Guinnessworldrecords.com. Retrieved February 23, 2019. http://www.guinnessworldrecords.com/world-records/93473-most-jumps-on-a-trampoline-grabbing-a-bar.

Hevesi, Dennis. "George Nissen, Father of the Trampoline, Dies at 96." *New York Times*, April 13, 2010. https://www.nytimes.com/2010/04/13/us/13nissen.html.

Hobson, Katherine. "As Trampoline Parks Jump in Popularity, So Do Injuries." NPR, August 1, 2016. https://www.npr.org/sections/health-shots/2016/08/01/487940627/as-trampoline-parks-jump-in-popularity-so-do-injuries.

Kennedy, John R. "Canada's Greg Roe Jumps into the Next Round of 'America's Got Talent.'" Global News, June 30, 2015. https://globalnews.ca/news/2085898/canadas-greg-roe-jumps-into-next-round-of-americas-got-talent.

Kennedy, Pagan. "Who Made That Trampoline?" *New York Times Magazine*, September 28, 2012. https://www.nytimes.com/2012/09/30/magazine/who-made-that-trampoline.html.

Maternowski, Todd. "The Roles of Spotters in Trampolining." AZCentral. Retrieved February 23, 2019. https://healthyliving.azcentral.com/roles-spotters-trampolining-12402.html.

NBC Olympics. Logan Dooley, biography. NBCOlympics, PyeongChang 2018. Retrieved March 4, 2019. http://archivepyc.nbcolympics.com/athletes/logan-dooley/664522.

NBC Olympics. Nicole Ahsinger, biography. NBCOlympics, PyeongChang 2018. Retrieved March 4, 2019. http://archivepyc.nbcolympics.com/athletes/nicole-ahsinger/1275207.

Proctor, Jason. "'They Are Very Dangerous': Trampoline Park Death Highlights Calls for Regulation." CBC, January 25, 2018. https://www.cbc.ca/news/canada/british-columbia/trampoline-injuries-death-regulation-1.4504378.

Rebounderz Indoor Trampoline Arena Extreme Fun Center. "Trampolines: A History." November 7, 2017. https://www.rebounderz.com/apopka/trampoline-parks-apopka/trampolines-a-history.

Reynolds, Adam. "The Benefits of Trampolining." Springfit Gymnastics and Trampoline Clubs. Retrieved February 23, 2019. https://springfit.org/activities/trampolining/benefits-of-trampolining.

Rosen, Ben. "Trampoline Injuries Soar Sky High: Are More Regulations Needed?" *Christian Science Monitor*, August 1, 2016. https://www.csmonitor.com/USA/2016/0801 /Trampoline-injuries-soar-sky-high-Are-more-regulations -needed.

Schwartz, Heather E. *Gymnastics.*Farmington Hills, MI: Gale, Cengage Learning, 2011.

Seninsky, Frank. "Trends Shaping the Amusement Industry: A Look at Trampoline Parks." *RePlay Magazine*, February 1, 2018. https://www.replaymag.com/frank-talk -february-2018.

Waters, Cara. "Keith Alexander's Invention Took 15 Years and Has Made $55 Million, but He Doesn't Own It." Stuff, December 18, 2017. https://www.stuff.co.nz/business /innovation/99942785/keith-alexanders-invention-took-15 -years-and-has-made-55-million-but-he-doesnt-own-it.

Welch, Ashley. "What's Behind a Big Jump in Trampoline Injuries?" CBS News, August 1, 2016. https://www .cbsnews.com/news/er-visits-jump-as-trampoline-parks -rise-in-popularity.

Wood, Stephanie. "Are Indoor Trampoline Parks Safe?" Safe Bee. Retrieved March 4, 2019. http://www.safebee.com /family/are-indoor-trampoline-parks-safe.

INDEX

ABOUT THE AUTHOR

Monique Vescia is the author of numerous nonfiction books on a variety of subjects, including *Extreme Parkour* (Extreme Sports and Stunts). She lives in Seattle with her husband and fellow writer, Don Rauf. Like George Nissen, inventor of the trampoline, she attended the University of Iowa.

PHOTO CREDITS

Cover, p. 1 Westend61Getty Images; cover, back cover, p. 1 (sky) Dove Lee/Moment/Getty Images; p. 5 Ronald Martinez/Getty Images; pp. 6, 11 Dean Mouhtaropoulos/Getty Images; p. 9 Bettmann/Getty Images; p. 13 Bridgeman Images; p. 15 frantic00/Shutterstock.com; p. 18 Bay Ismoyo/AFP/Getty Images; pp. 20, 33 Visual China Group/Getty Images; p. 21 Nathan Stirk/Getty Images; p. 23 Matthias Hangst/Getty Images; p. 26 Mars0hod/Shutterstock.com; p. 28 Sergii Sobolevskyi/Shutterstock.com; p. 29 Steve Mann/Shutterstock.com; p. 31 Kazuhiro Nogi/AFP/Getty Images; p. 35 David Ramos/Getty Images; interior pages (jumping silhouette) www.iStock.com/Nosyrevy.

Design and Layout: Michael Moy; Photo Researcher: Sherri Jackson